P9-DMZ-384

3 1668 02937 8848

DEC 3 1 2002

Summerglen Branch Library

CHILDREN 92 FRASER
Morrison, Taylor.
The buffalo nickel /

The Buffalo Nickel

HOUGHTON MIFFLIN COMPANY BOSTON 2002 Walter Lorraine (wℓ) Books

For Thomas Sgouros

Copyright © 2002 by Taylor Morrison

All rights reserved. For information about permission to reproduce selections
from this book, write to Permissions, Houghton Mifflin Company, 215 Park
Avenue South, New York, New York 10003.
www.houghtonmifflinbooks.com

Library of Congress Cataloging-in-Publication Data
Morrison, Taylor.
  The buffalo nickel / Taylor Morrison.
    p. cm.
Includes bibliographical references.
  Summary: A biography of the sculptor of the buffalo nickel, who
grew up in the Dakota Territory where Sioux children were his
playmates, buffalo robes were his blankets, and the town whittler
was his art teacher.
  ISBN 0-618-10855-6
  1. Fraser, James Earle, 1876–1953—Juvenile literature. 2. Sculptors—
United States—Biography—Juvenile literature. 3. Coin design—United
States—Juvenile literature. 4. Mints—United States—Juvenile
literature. 5. Nickel (Coin)—Juvenile literature. [1. Fraser, James Earle,
1876–1953. 2. Sculptors. 3. Coins. 4. Money.] I. Title.
NB237.F67 M67 2002
730'.92—dc21
[B]   2001039537

Printed in the United States of America
WOZ 10 9 8 7 6 5 4 3 2 1

The Buffalo Nickel

Taylor Morrison

FORT WORTH PUBLIC LIBRARY

In 1880, Thomas and Cora Fraser moved their family from Minnesota to the town of Mitchell in the Dakota Territory. Thomas was a mechanical engineer working for the Chicago, Milwaukee & St. Paul railroad. They were building a line from Sanborn, Iowa, to Deadwood in the Black Hills. The Frasers lived in a boxcar at first. It was a reasonably comfortable home except for the occasional jolts from the switch engine. Thomas was often away working on the railroad, so Cora spent a lot of time with their four-year-old son and baby girl. The boy, James, would gaze at the prairie from the boxcar door. The howling winds and vast, flat plain made him feel lonely and homesick.

The Frasers moved into a ranch house after several months in the train yard. The winter brought dangerous blizzards. The freezing wind blew relentlessly. Their unfinished home often had several inches of snow on the floor.

There were few other children to play with, so James spent most of his time alone. He watched the flocks of geese return in the spring and the noisy bustling of prairie chickens. Wildlife was abundant on the prairie. Small groups of antelope and wolves would often pass by.

The rugged Dakota Territory changed rapidly as the years passed. Settlers were turning the wild prairie into farmland. Prairie schooners, full of restless people heading west in search of a new life, would regularly pass the Frasers' house.

James heard many stories from his elders of the way the prairie used to be. An old trapper who spent winters with the Indians would occasionally visit James's grandfather. He told incredible stories of great herds of buffalo that stretched on for miles. He also described the Indians who hunted the powerful buffalo and depended on them for food.

Occasionally, a few families of Sioux Indians would leave their reservations when they became restless. James would be awakened by barking dogs, and from his window he would see a camp of tepees set up near their ranch home. The Sioux children showed James how to play their games. They taught him how to make arrows from cattails in a pond. Then they would shoot frogs as they stuck their heads out of the water. Later on they would use the frogs to make soup.

Unfortunately, the camps were only temporary. Soldiers would encourage the families to return to their reservations after a few days of hunting.

One morning at sunrise James saw a Sioux shaman dressed in strips of buffalo hide. He was praying for the return of the buffalo herds.

The buffalo were in the way of the railroads being built. They were also easy targets for the hide hunters and had been nearly exterminated. Long white trails of bones were the only remnants of the great herds.

James was exposed to many forms of art. He loved to watch his father sketch inventions to improve the railroad. There were the painted tepees and bright costumes of the Sioux. Colorful designs were painted on the soft buffalo robes that he and his little sister liked to play on.

After school James would rush home to watch the town whittler, a hunchback, carve on his porch. He skillfully carved a round ball surrounded by pillars from a block of chalkstone. James was inspired. He found some pieces of chalkstone at the local quarry and began carving little sculptures of animals and people.

James's grandfather bartered with a Sioux chief to get James a pony. The young bronco was named Billy, and he was very feisty. When James tried to ride, Billy would buck him off and rear up, trying to kick him. James learned to control Billy by carrying a long spear and a whip. A pack of dogs James had adopted followed them on their daily adventures. When his father announced that they were moving again, James was filled with grief. He had grown to love the land, animals, and contact with the Sioux in his prairie home.

The Frasers moved to Chicago after spending a year in Minnesota. James began working in a sculptor's studio and taking night classes at the Art Institute of Chicago. In 1893, when James was seventeen, the Columbian Exposition was held in Chicago. People from all over the world came to see the grand architecture and giant sculptures on display. The fair inspired James to create *The End of the Trail,* a depiction of an exhausted brave on a weary horse. The sculpture was based on a sad phrase he remembered about the Sioux being moved west, away from their homelands: "The Indians will be pushed into the Pacific Ocean."

Thomas Fraser was worried that James would become a starving artist, but a friend and art collector reviewed his work and convinced Thomas that James was extremely talented. Obtaining his father's permission, he traveled overseas to study at the great art schools in Paris. *The End of the Trail* won him $1,000 in a contest for American artists. It also won the admiration of the famous sculptor Augustus Saint-Gaudens, who invited James to work in his studio. The master sculptor was working on a giant equestrian monument to General William Tecumseh Sherman. James learned many new skills and developed great work habits in Saint-Gaudens's busy studio.

When the monument was completed in 1902, James knew it was time to set off on his own. He had worked for four years in Saint-Gaudens's incredible studio, and they remained close friends. James set up his own studio in MacDougal Alley, a small artist's colony in New York City. There he befriended many artists and began to receive work.

In 1905, President Theodore Roosevelt hired Augustus Saint-Gaudens to create some American coins with the high raised relief of ancient Greek coins. The elderly Saint-Gaudens died before he could see his beautiful ten- and twenty-dollar gold coins minted in 1907. The great sculptor was the first independent artist to design a coin. Now the door was open for other artists.

In 1909, Victor Brenner's extremely popular Lincoln cent was created. The public and the government soon turned their attention to changing the nickel. Only after twenty-five years could a coin design be changed, and the old liberty nickel's lifespan had expired. In the spring of 1911, James pursued the opportunity to create a new nickel. He thought a plains Indian chief and a buffalo were distinctly American. They would be linked on the two sides of the coin as they were linked together in life. James combined the features of three famous chiefs for the Indian head: Two Moons, Iron Tail, and Big Tree. The chiefs visited New York City and posed for him.

First, the artist sketched many ideas.

A wooden base for a clay model was prepared.

The clay background was flattened.

The drawing was transferred onto the clay.

James used a buffalo named Black Diamond at the Central Park Zoo for a model. Black Diamond became annoyed at James's constant staring and refused to face the right way.

James worked furiously. He showed many different drawings and models to the officials of the Mint and the Treasury. In January 1912, the secretary of the Treasury, Franklin MacVeagh, finally selected James as the artist to create the new nickel.

Wet plaster was poured onto
the clay model to make a plaster cast.

When the plaster had dried,
a negative plaster cast was carefully lifted off.

A positive cast was then
made from the negative, and
the tiny details were touched up.

James worked into the summer perfecting the plaster models. He worked closely with a friend named Henri Weil, who ran the Medallic Art Company in New York City. Weil owned a special machine called a Janvier lathe. The lathe could reduce the designs on the plaster models down five times, to the size of a nickel. Weil helped James see what the experimental coin would eventually look like. He made small silver-plated models called galvanotrials. MacVeagh and many prominent artists on the Fine Arts Commission, such as Daniel Chester French, enthusiastically praised the new nickel design. They had to approve it before it went into mass production.

Things were going very smoothly until a company called Hobbs Manufacturing interfered. The owners complained that the relief, or raised design, on the buffalo nickel was too high to fit into the slot machines they were about to produce. The director of the Mint, George Roberts, urged James to work with the company. James was angry because he wanted to make the relief on the coin fuller and richer than the old, flat Liberty nickel. After several months MacVeagh realized that no compromise could be reached between the artist and the industry, so he pushed for final approval of James's designs.

James's final designs were prepared for the Mint at the Medallic Art Company. The plaster models of the nickel were cast in bronze to give them a hard surface. Then the bronze castings were placed on the Janvier lathe.

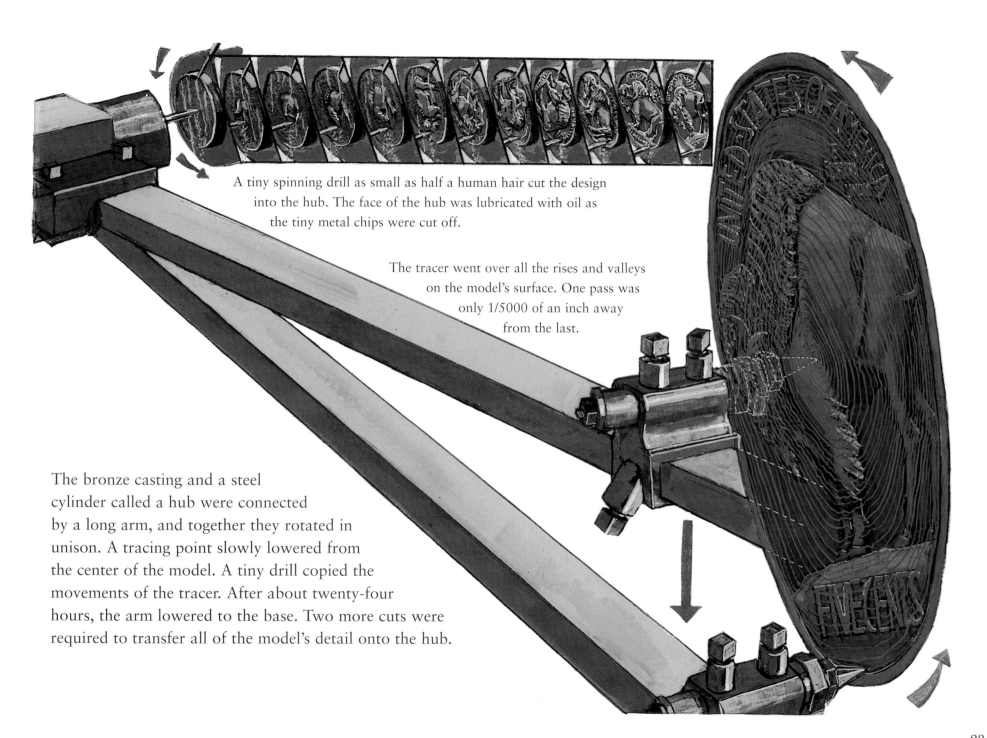

A tiny spinning drill as small as half a human hair cut the design into the hub. The face of the hub was lubricated with oil as the tiny metal chips were cut off.

The tracer went over all the rises and valleys on the model's surface. One pass was only 1/5000 of an inch away from the last.

The bronze casting and a steel cylinder called a hub were connected by a long arm, and together they rotated in unison. A tracing point slowly lowered from the center of the model. A tiny drill copied the movements of the tracer. After about twenty-four hours, the arm lowered to the base. Two more cuts were required to transfer all of the model's detail onto the hub.

The pair of master hubs were sent to the U.S. Mint in Philadelphia. The hubs were used to make negative copies called dies. The master die was used to make working hubs, which were then used to make working dies. The working dies would eventually stamp the coins.

Mass production of the buffalo nickel was delayed into 1913. James struggled to keep his patience as the Hobbs Company relentlessly demanded that he flatten and alter his designs. On February 14, a final meeting was held in MacVeagh's office in Washington to sort out the controversy.

The master hubs were hardened by heating them in a furnace and then dunking them in water.

A hub was placed in a powerful press and squashed into an annealed die blank. The cone of the die filled all the crevices in the hub.

The great pressure deformed the die, so the excess steel was cut away on a lathe. The working dies were then shaped to fit into the coining presses.

The meeting was crowded with people arguing about the new nickel: MacVeagh, Roberts, representatives from the Hobbs Company, several lawyers, and James. After the meeting, MacVeagh wrote a letter to Roberts, stating that the artistic beauty of the coin was more important than the requirements of a machine. The machine should be changed and not the artwork. He concluded by saying, "You will please, therefore, proceed with the coinage of the new nickel." James was relieved to receive a telegram the next day that stated the ruling was in his favor.

On February 17, 1913, the Mint began producing thousands of the new nickels.

A molten alloy of copper and nickel was poured into ingot molds. The ingot was then rolled down to a sheet the thickness of a nickel. Blanks were cut from the strip, and their edges were raised to help the flow of metal during stamping. Next they were annealed and cleaned.

The blanks were fed through tubes into the coining presses. Metal fingers dropped a blank into a collar on top of the lower die. The upper die then hammered the blank against the lower die. Next the fingers ejected the stamped coin.

27

On February 22, a canvas bag full of the first buffalo nickels was brought to Fort Wadsworth in Staten Island, New York. President Taft and many important chiefs were attending a ceremony to inaugurate a memorial to the American Indian. A giant bronze statue of a chief, almost as tall as the Statue of Liberty, was going to be placed on top of the fort. After a flag–raising ceremony, the new nickels were given out to everyone present. The buffalo nickel was very popular with the public. In cities around the country, people waited in long lines to get the new nickels.

That same year, James married a sculptor named Laura Gardin. The couple moved to a studio in Connecticut and spent a lifetime together creating beautiful medals and monuments.

The giant memorial at Fort Wadsworth was never built for unknown reasons, but James's nickel stayed in circulation for twenty-five years. His powerful artwork remained an honorable memorial to an animal that nearly became extinct and a race of people whose way of life was rapidly vanishing.

ACKNOWLEDGMENTS

Many people and institutions helped me piece together this story of American art and history. I would like to thank D. Wayne Johnson, numismatic researcher and writer, for giving me valuable research materials and answering many of my questions; Tim Grant, Edgar Steever, and the workers of the United States Mint in Philadelphia for demonstrating the steps involved in minting coins and showing me an original 1912 bronze buffalo nickel model; Douglas A. Mudd at the Smithsonian Institution; Monique Evans Westcott at the Community College of Philadelphia; Tom Kavanaugh at William Hammond Mathers Museum; the librarians of special collections at the George Arents Library of Syracuse University; the National Sculpture Society; the Free Library of Philadelphia; Mike Ryan at Fort Wadsworth; Paul Woehrmann at the Milwaukee Public Library; Anne Wheeler at the Cowboy Hall of Fame; Laurie Holmberg at the Middle Border Museum; Mary Edwards at the Department of the Treasury; Francis D. Campbell at the American Numismatic Society; Gregory Schwarz and Henry Duffy at the Saint-Gaudens National Historic Site; and Joe Rust and Ron Landis at the Gallery Mint museum for explaining how a blank is prepared for stamping, how a die is prepared, and how a knuckle coining press works. Also, thank you to David for his criticism and to Walt and Erv for finding me models.

BIBLIOGRAPHY

Alexander, David T. "Fraser's Plasters Find Collector Marketplace." *Coin World*, October 15, 1980.

Augustus Saint-Gaudens 1848–1907: A Master of American Sculpture. Toulouse: Musée des Augustins, 1999.

Barber, Charles. "Preparing Coin Dies." *Numismatic Scrapbook*, October 1951.

———. The letters of Chief Engraver Charles Barber 1911–1915. U.S. Mint, Philadelphia.

Breen, Walter. *Walter Breen's Complete Encyclopedia of U.S. and Colonial Coins*. New York: Doubleday, 1988.

Bressett, Kenneth. *A Guide Book of United States Coins*. New York: St. Martin's Press, 2000.

Cohen, Annette R., and Ray M. Druley. *The Buffalo Nickel*. Arlington, Va.: Potomac Enterprises, 1979.

Fraser, James Earle. Unpublished autobiography, papers, and photos. George Arents Library, Syracuse University. Syracuse, N.Y.

———. The American Heritage in Sculpture. James Earle Fraser Estate, Syracuse University Art Collection, Thomas Gilcrease Institute of American History and Art, 1985.

Hassrick, Royal B. *The Sioux: Life and Customs of a Warrior Society*. Norman: University of Oklahoma Press, 1964.

Hoskins, Charles R. "The Coin That Never Was: The 1912 Buffalo Nickel." *Numorum*, Spring 1978.

"Indians See Taft Handle Spade." *New York Times*, February 23, 1913.

Johnson, D. Wayne. "Home of the Art Medal." *Coinage*, December 1967.

———. "The Medal Maker: Master Sculptor Laura Gardin Fraser." Medallic Art Company & Mike Craven Productions, 1997. Videocassette.

Krakel, Dean. *End of the Trail: The Odyssey of a Statue*. Norman: University of Oklahoma Press, 1973.

Lange, David W. *The Complete Guide to Buffalo Nickels*. 2nd edition. Virginia Beach, Va.: DLRC Press, 2000.

Loucheim, Aline B. "Most Famous Unknown Sculptor." *New York Times Magazine*, May 13, 1951.

"New York Artist Who Designed New Nickel." *Brooklyn Daily Eagle*, March 9, 1913.

Ratzman, Leonard J. "The Buffalo Nickel: A 50-Year-Old Mystery." *Whitman Numismatic Journal*, May 1, 1964.

Reed, Fred L. "The Frasers, Married Collaborators, Left Their Mark on the Nation's Coinage in Remarkable Ways." *Coin World*, January 5, 1998.

Reed, Mort. *Cowles Complete Encyclopedia of U.S. Coins*. New York: Cowles Book Co., 1969.

Taxay, Don. *The U.S. Mint and Coinage*. New York: Arco Publishing, 1966.

Thompson, Walter. "The Working Die and Our Coinage." *Numismatic Scrapbook*, August 1959.

Van Ryzin, Robert R. "The Real Indian Models." *Coins*, October 1994.

Young, James Rankin. *The United States Mint at Philadelphia*. Philadelphia, 1903.

GLOSSARY

ALLOY: A combination of metals melted together. The buffalo nickel was 75 percent copper and 25 percent nickel.

ANNEAL: To soften metal by heating it and then cooling it slowly.

BIG TREE: A Kiowa chief who was also called Adoeette.

BRENNER, VICTOR DAVID: The designer of the Lincoln cent.

BUFFALO ROBE: A blanket made of a buffalo hide. The inside was decorated with vibrant, symbolic paintings.

CHALKSTONE: A soft, yellow stone found by riverbanks in southern South Dakota.

CHICAGO, MILWAUKEE & ST. PAUL RAILROAD: The company that was building lines across South Dakota and Minnesota in the 1880s.

CLAY MODEL: A flat clay base on which medalists modeled forms and letters.

COINING PRESS: The machine that stamped the designs from the die into the blanks.

COLLAR: A steel cylinder that held a blank in place as it was stamped in the press.

DIE: A tool with the negative relief of the coin design, used to strike blanks.

FORT WADSWORTH: An old army fort, first used in the Revolutionary War to defend New York Harbor.

FRASER, JAMES EARLE: One of America's greatest unknown sculptors and medalists. His work was extremely popular, and it is still copied and reproduced today.

FRASER, LAURA GARDIN: A prominent and extremely versatile sculptor. She created medallions, giant history panels, and monuments.

FRENCH, DANIEL CHESTER: A great sculptor known for his seated Lincoln in the Lincoln Memorial.

GALVANOTRIAL: A wax proof of a coin or medal design that is coated first with copper, then with a thin layer of electroplated silver.

HARDEN: To heat steel until it is bright red and then dunk it in water to cool it quickly.

HOBBS COMPANY: The manufacturers of vending machines that detected fake coins.

HUB: A tool containing a positive impression of a coin design, used to make a die.

INGOT: A bar of metal formed in a mold from molten metal.

IRON TAIL: An Oglala Sioux chief who fought at Little Big Horn.

JANVIER (zhan-vee-ay) LATHE: A three-dimensional pantograph invented by Victor Janvier in 1892. The Mint still uses one that is one-hundred years old.

LIBERTY NICKEL: Designed in 1883 by the Mint's chief engraver, Charles Barber.

LATHE: A machine that spins and cuts metal objects. Lathes are used to turn dies so they are the correct shape to fit in a coining press.

MEDALLIC ART COMPANY: A company created in 1909 by two brothers, Henri and Felix Weil. Its purpose was to assist artists by reducing and enlarging their work with special machines brought from France.

PLASTER MODEL: A cast of a clay model made from a paste of gypsum and water.

RELIEF: A type of sculpture with forms projecting from a flat surface.

ROOSEVELT, THEODORE: The twenty-sixth president of the United States. He was disgusted with the ugliness of U.S. coins and directed the Mint to make beautiful, high-relief coins.

SAINT-GAUDENS, AUGUSTUS: The first independent artist to design a U.S. coin. His twenty-dollar gold piece is considered to be the most beautiful coin ever made by the Mint. Saint-Gaudens taught many students who later designed U.S. coins, including Fraser.

SHAMAN: A holy man who healed people, led ceremonies, and had close contact with the spirit world.

SHERMAN MONUMENT: A memorial to the Civil War general William Tecumseh Sherman. It stands in Grand Army Plaza in New York City.

SIOUX: A general name given to several groups of plains Indians who speak similar languages. They were buffalo hunters and brave warriors.

TEPEE: A portable shelter built by tribes of plains Indians and made of many buffalo hides.

TWO MOONS: A Northern Cheyenne Chief.

WORLD'S COLUMBIAN EXPOSITION: A world's fair in Chicago in 1893 featuring an exhibition of classical architecture and sculpture.